IMPOSSIBLE TO FORGET

Living with Anti-Semitism

By

J. J. Patrick

authorHOUSE

1663 LIBERTY DRIVE, SUITE 200
BLOOMINGTON, INDIANA 47403
(800) 839-8640
www.authorhouse.com

First published by AuthorHouse 07/14/04

ISBN: 1-4184-6134-2 (e)
ISBN: 1-4184-6135-0 (sc)

This book is printed on acid-free paper.

Printed in the United States of America
Bloomington, Indiana

To my precious husband, Charles, who has continually--and without complaint--supported me through our forty-nine years of marriage, and allowed me to pursue one dream after another. This is the latest.

I LOVE YOU

A WORD OF SINCERE THANKS

In 1994, I was a student of the Institute of Children's Literature, and wrote a non-fiction Essay, consisting of approximately 1200 words, as one of my assignments.

It was a wonderful course, and I had a wonderful instructor, Connie Hiser, who wrote on my returned graded assignment,

"This cries out to be a book. I'd love to see you expand on this!"

Well, here it is, ten years later--Expanded. Though the story is still painful, it is true; unfortunately, the choking hands of Anti-Semitism are still pervasive in our country today.

To my wonderful friend and mentor--and constant supporter, Tracie McLean of AuthorHouse, who has assisted me, <u>every step of the way!</u>

To a very incredibly talented Angelique McLean, who designed the Cover of my book. When I first saw it, I thought, My story could stink, but the Cover would surely sell!

And last but not least, to my Editor and Typist,

B.J. Seaman, who graciously corrected my bad English and punctuation.

Thank you ALL so very much

PROLOGUE

At the age of thirteen, I was beginning my freshman year at a high school in Southern California. Up to this point in time, I was a very well adjusted student, making good grades, and had many friends. Though I had read and vaguely knew about anti-Semitism--and what it meant--it had not affected my family or me. I was totally unprepared for the antagonism, cruelty and prejudice that I was subjected to every day, during the time I spent at that school.

I shed many tears, and I kept these problems to myself as long as I could. In actuality, I stayed at this high school through my freshman year and the first semester of my sophomore year. But by that time, I was ill, my doctor's requests were not honored, my grades and health were failing, and my parents finally had to know of the circumstances. I have never seen such rage in my father. He threatened the school with exposure by the newspapers, and a lawsuit; consequently, I was released from there within minutes!

It took some years to put this story into book form, even though the book is small in pages--it is large in substance. I needed to bring forth the terrible remembrances of a young, naïve and sheltered girl, experiencing her first and painful taste of hatred, called anti-Semitism.

Everything in the story is true, with the exception of names and locations. It is only a "miniscule" sampling of what I endured for one and one-half years--and impossible to write every single thing that happened to me on a daily basis. From that time to present date, I still hurt when I think of those experiences, and will never understand why this had to be--and often wonder if this particular school still suffers from such protagonism and ignorance.

I have spent many years in the medical field, and have witnessed many surgeries. And guess what? We are ALL IDENTICAL INSIDE!!

TABLE OF CONTENTS

CHAPTER ONE

What a terrible morning. It was the second week of September, and the day was already hot and sticky. Now Anna was on her way to high school, and had spent the whole morning arguing with her parents. This was nothing new; she was always arguing with her parents. This particular argument was about the way she looked, and it was truly bad! But she couldn't help it, and tried to explain to her very old-fashioned and strict parents that she had absolutely no control over her appearance. She had been ordered to dress this way by the upper classmen at her high school, due to the rules of Freshman Initiation. She couldn't believe how much she had looked forward to beginning her freshman year, and now this.

The first week was getting the correct classes, learning her way around campus, and getting acclimated to a longer and more stringent educational environment. She'd had it so easy in grade school that she was a bit bewildered by this big change in her life. She tried to tell her parents that the entire freshman class had to dress this way for the whole second week of school. This first week of school was also a great disappointment. She didn't see too many of her friends from grade school, and was upset by some of the students making fun of her, and asking, "What are you doing in this school? Don't your synagogues have any high school for you to attend?"

She thought, Synagogues? Why on earth would I belong to a Synagogue? I'm not Jewish, I'm Catholic!

However, as the first week progressed, she noticed that her teachers looked at her strangely, and were not as helpful and supportive to her as they were to other beginning students. Her classmates also seemed to distance themselves from her. Only a few spoke to her, and that made her feel like a true outsider, and she couldn't understand why. She soon realized that this was only the beginning of a long siege of mindless intolerance that she would be subjected to, because it seemed as though everyone thought that she was a Jew.

She wasn't Jewish, but so what? Why all of this animosity? The war was over, and she was here to learn, just like everyone else. But after the first week, she was literally afraid of this second week of school, which was Freshman Initiation. She had already experienced strong animosity toward her in the previous week. She didn't want to think that the word <u>scared</u> applied to her state of mind, but in many ways, yes, she had to admit that she was scared. She hoped that the abuses would remain verbal, like, "Hey Jew girl, what are you doing here? You don't belong here!" Or, "Where did you get that big nose? Can you dig dirt with it?"

These terrible, cruel, outlandish remarks made her extremely nervous and jittery all the time. She couldn't figure out whom she could talk to, if anyone, and if she could talk to someone, what would she say? She was afraid to voice her concerns to anyone, for fear of retaliation. She never knew what to expect from one minute to the next.

She also wasn't anywhere near to being prepared for the tough classes that her father had managed to assign to her. The "3 R's" in grade school had been a snap, and everything had been so easy. She wondered if her friends were having the same difficulty that she was. She had never been very good at Math, but always managed to get by. Now, she had Algebra. My God, she thought, how am I going to handle <u>that</u> class? Her father had set up the classes that she should take: Latin, Algebra, World History, English, and not to forget P.E.—Phys. Education. Thank God for a Study Hall. World History she liked, and felt that she could handle that subject OK; and English--well, she always excelled in English, so she wasn't worried about that either. Then came Latin. This course made her consider running away from school. Maybe even home.

Anna asked her father, "Why Latin? Nobody speaks Latin. In this state, California, the second language is Spanish. If you're looking for a job, the employers always want you to be bilingual, which is Spanish. So why can't I take Spanish?"

"Because," her father said, "Latin is the basis of all languages, beginning with English. You may decide to become a nurse one day, and you'll need Latin."

Anna thought, Right! What a ridiculous conversation this is. And where did he get all of this wrong information? Shows you how much <u>he</u> knows.

She didn't know why she had to take all of these college preparatory classes, when she was never going to be allowed to go to college. When she argued about this with her father, he said, "We'll see." End of conversation.

Anna Balak was of Egyptian descent, and though her parents were born in the United States, her paternal and maternal grandparents arrived in the U.S. from Cairo in 1924. Even though they were now Americans, her culture considered a woman's role to be raising children and keeping a good home. <u>Barefoot and pregnant</u> was their way of life.

This hadn't changed much when Anna celebrated her thirteenth birthday. Her mother was uneducated, as were her aunts, uncles, and cousins. Even her father was a self-made businessman without formal education. Therefore, she considered all of the college prep courses a waste of time. She really wanted business courses: shorthand, typing, economics, etc. Her father understood business, so maybe he'd change his mind later on.

CHAPTER TWO

Anna looked straight ahead through the car window as her father pulled up and stopped in front of the high school. She hated the fact that he had to take her to school every morning. She took the school bus home everyday after school, and it stopped about two blocks from her home. But in the mornings, the closest the bus came to her home was about a mile, and with her books, was too long a walk. Now, it was Monday morning of the second week of school, and the beginning of Freshman Initiation on campus. The freshmen were told by the upper classmen that they had to be obedient and "do everything that the upper classmen requested of them." Also, "They would answer to the word <u>slave</u> at all times, because that is what they were."

Anna hoped that it wasn't going to be too strenuous, and had absolutely no idea how bad it was really going to get. Well, right now, she looked forward to the end of the week, because Friday would be the finish of this madness called "Initiation".

"See you later, Dad." Without looking at him, she opened the car door.

"Anna, look at me when you speak to me. How do you think I feel, raising a lovely daughter, and allowing her to go to school looking like a stupid, penniless street urchin?"

Anna turned and looked at her father. She watched him grimace as he looked at her. His dark eyes were stern. Her father could sometimes be supportive, but he was also very old-fashioned in his ways, and couldn't comprehend the reasoning behind Freshman Initiation. Well, neither could she.

"Dad, for the thousandth time, there's nothing I can do about this. It's school rules, and all of the freshmen have to go through this misery for a whole week! It probably happens to all freshmen starting at every high school around here. Do you think I enjoy this? I can hardly wait until it's over! Please, no more arguing. That's all we've been doing all morning, and it's already given me a giant headache and ruined my day. I'll see you after school."

She stepped out of the car, slamming the door behind her. As her father drove away, she felt relief and apprehension at the same time. Dear God, she thought, it isn't enough that I have to look like something out of a horror movie for a whole week. If Dad knew what was REALLY troubling me, he'd probably tear this place apart.

Nothing was going right. She could hardly believe that this was what she had been dreaming about and looking forward to for at least two years. As a female in a Middle Eastern family, once you've reached puberty, you were constantly kept under close watch by your parents. Therefore, the freedom of play and puppy-love-boyfriends was definitely over. Parents got extremely overprotective, and all of a sudden, life got very restricted. No more movie nights with your girlfriends; no more sleep-overs or slumber parties at their homes--even if their parents were present at all times. The books you read were governed, as were the movies and phone calls. At that time, parents were still arranging marriages for their daughters. She was suffering growing pains at home. So, when anticipating the liberalness that high school would bring, she was absolutely ecstatic, knowing that, at least in high school, her restrictiveness would be over. Consequently, she was certainly not prepared for the way that she would be accepted. Anna never figured on being scared every day at school. Who would? She was really a very nice, innocent, and vulnerable young girl; and never, ever, argued with classmates. This was a totally different, fearful atmosphere.

CHAPTER THREE

The year was 1945, World War II had ended, and anti-Semitism was very prevalent in the United States.

Anna had grown up in a very small town, where her parents had owned and operated a mercantile store; and had attended the town's public elementary school- -first through eighth grades. There was also a Lutheran elementary school, where some of her friends attended. Everyone in town knew everyone else, where they lived, and their children. The comfort of growing up with friends for eight plus years, who were almost like siblings, was absolutely wonderful for her; and she missed those days so much. Now, she saw only a few of her friends maybe once a week, and none shared any classes with her. The expectation of going to high school had kept her awake many nights. She had been so excited, and had felt so grown up, even though she was only thirteen.

She did have a "first love" in grade school for two years; and they had been very attentive and supportive of one another. But after graduation, his family moved to another state. Though they communicated by mail for a while; and professed their "dying love", they never saw each other again, which delighted Anna's parents.

Her growing-up years were really quite uneventful. Her mother and father worked diligently in their mercantile store to support their family, which consisted of Anna and a younger brother. While very young, she and her brother were taught to "help out" in the store: weigh and bag vegetables for the produce stand, dust the canned goods, shelves and counters, pick up all trash on the sidewalk in front of the store, and sweep the floors every night. By the time Anna was twelve, she was cashing large payroll checks.

This is synonymous with the raising of children in foreign families. However, while <u>very</u> young, there was always plenty of time for play. Her parents sold their store the year before Anna started high school, which was 1944.

Anna was very proud of her parents, and they were also very respected by the community. When they had the store, they always took care of the town's needs when asked; and it was sometimes very difficult to do during the wartime "rationing" years. Her father was also on the School Board of the Public School; and during the war, was the Air-Raid Warden, in charge of security for their small community. To her knowledge, her family never--at any time--suffered from prejudice or any injustice because of their race, even though there were many German families in town--most of them, customers in the store. So, she was very unready for the onslaught of her current situation at school.

Now, unfortunately, to Anna's dismay and fears, the high school that she was attending was in another small, but predominately German town; and the majority of teachers in the high school were of German descent, as were most of the students. The town had four Lutheran elementary schools, so the majority of the students came to this one and only high school. She had already been exposed to the antagonism and prejudice by her teachers--from Day One--along with jeers and snide remarks from some of the students, mostly male. She was beginning to feel very lost, alone, and fearful in this hateful arena. She had so looked forward to the freedom of high school, because everything was so regimented at home; but nothing could have prepared her for this type of animosity and cruelty. This was something that scared her, and she had been totally unaware of its ugly existence. She had no idea, nor preparedness for the persecution that would follow her during her freshman year, and the first semester of her sophomore year.

Anna had an olive complexion, synonymous with Middle Eastern heritage, and large facial features--dark hair, dark eyes--which were being mistaken for <u>Jewish</u> heritage. There were some junior and senior students in the high school who knew Anna very well. But now, in this environment, they chose to ignore her. They weren't in any way abusive, just frightfully aloof. Their parents had been customers in her parent's store, and they lived in the same small town. Anna grew up with them. This hurt Anna very much. If she saw one of these students on campus and said "Hi," that person would ignore her.

Anna learned that during the past war years, a feeling of unrest among the students had permeated the campus, and because of wartime restrictions, school activities were greatly curtailed. But this year, 1945, the school saw the return of a freer atmosphere, the revival of many campus activities such as Freshman Initiation, and a new attitude toward anyone who looked different.

Well, here comes Anna Balak, and she certainly looked different. She didn't look German, her skin was the wrong color--olive toned--and she had a big nose. Didn't Jews have big noses? And because her parents were so strict and old-fashioned, she couldn't rid herself of the black hair on her legs, arms, and upper lip. Her dark eyebrows were too thick, because she wasn't allowed to pluck them, and she wasn't allowed to wear lipstick or makeup of any kind. Consequently, she didn't look like any other girl on campus. Different? You bet. Instead of feeling sorry for her, these ignorant students and teachers decided to persecute her. After all, she was just a "filthy, scummy Jew," wasn't she? And that's how everyone continued to refer to her.

CHAPTER FOUR

Anna walked briskly into the mathematics building and pushed open the door of the ladies room. She was so glad the room was empty. She walked up to the full-length mirror and looked at herself. She felt like throwing up, and the tears formed in her large dark eyes. How is it possible that anyone can be made to look so ugly? Her clear olive complexion was completely covered with heavy white cold cream, and her face was totally devoid of any makeup. Her dark hair was done up in tight little pin curls flat against her head, and without the benefit of a scarf or bandana. Her plaid skirt and polka-dot blouse were inside out and backwards. She wore a different sock color on each foot, and mismatched shoes. She stood not quite five feet tall, and was overweight by about twenty pounds. The tears that had formed in her lovely dark eyes bubbled over. She knew she was certainly no beauty, but she could hardly bear the humiliation of this and the constant degradation leveled at the freshman by all of the upper classmen. She picked up her books, walked out into the hallway, and headed for her first class.

"Hey, slave, I need some help with these books!"

Anna knew that voice. Clay Mitchell. What a way to start a day. She already had a full-blown headache, from arguing with her parents before school.

When Anna first saw Clay, she had thought he was the most handsome boy she'd ever seen. He was tall and muscular, and one of the school's top athletes. His blond hair was cut very short, and he had the most gorgeous blue-green eyes. Then, to Anna's dismay, she had overheard him utter an obscenity to a lowly freshman, and she realized that his great appearance couldn't possibly compensate for his vulgarity and rudeness.

Anna turned and faced him. "I've got to get to class, Clay. If I carry your books, I'll be late to class and I'll get a demerit."

"Too bad, slave, you know the rules. You lowlies have to submit to the upper classmen at all times." He piled five large books onto her outstretched arms and said, "Let's go, slave."

Anna immediately felt the pain in her arms, shoulders, thighs and lower back. She knew that she shouldn't be doing this, and could hardly bear the weight of the additional burden, as she followed him upstairs to his classroom.

Inside, he directed her to his desk, and in the midst of a whole classroom of students, said, "Thanks, Ugly. Are all Jews as ugly as you?"

There wasn't a teacher in the classroom yet, so the students enjoyed the oppressive remarks by Clay. Would he have said them if a teacher had been in the room? With what Anna had already gone through the past week and a half, she didn't know and was afraid to speculate.

Anna dumped Clay's books on his desk, and, hearing muffled laughter in the classroom, felt the white heat of rage consume her. She picked her own books from his desk and staggered to the classroom door. She could hardly see her way for the tears in her eyes, as she stumbled down the stairs and ran to her math class. She was so grateful that she didn't let Clay and those other miserable students see her cry. She couldn't believe the meanness of it all. During that second week of school, she calculated that she had carried about four-hundred books that belonged to upper classmen. No wonder her back hurt so much.

"You're seven minutes late, Miss Balak," her teacher told her, "and the second bell has rung. You know what that means."

Anna looked at Mrs. Schultz and knew that her pleas would fall on deaf ears. The classroom turned instantly quiet. Mrs. Schultz was a large woman who wore no makeup, and her grey hair was pulled taut into a bun at the back of her head. Her slanted blue eyes were stern and angry, looking down at Anna. Her size and demeanor made her intimidating to her students, especially if she didn't like them.

"Mrs. Schultz, I was forced to be late; I had to carry Clay Mitchell's books to his upstairs classroom."

"No excuses, Anna. The upper classmen know they cannot make a freshman late for class. <u>You people</u> always have excuses for everything. You all think that your are above reproach. Go and see Mrs. Heinrich in the Attendance Office."

Anna felt crushed. She turned and walked out the door, wondering how she would explain to her parents the demerit she was surely going to get. She could already hear the yelling when she told them the reason for the demerit. It seemed that no matter what she did, it was never good enough or accepted by anyone at that school. She was so disheartened most of the time, which made it difficult for her to get a handle on her studies, and she had so much homework every day. She was so used to the friendly and laughing camaderie that she had shared with her friends and elementary school classmates. But where were they? She hardly ever saw them anymore, and could really use a good laugh and hug during this stressful time.

When Anna got to the Attendance Office, she found Mrs. Heinrich alone. She was certainly grateful for that, since she'd had students laughing at her all morning.

Mrs. Heinrich was tall and lanky, with short cropped grey hair, and small, narrow blue eyes that looked at you as though you were certainly guilty of something. Anna always thought that Mrs. Heinrich reminded her of the witch in the Snow White movie. She had that same pinched, ugly, distrustful expression, and she always acted as though she would really like to see you disappear.

She looked up at Anna from her desk and asked, "May I help you with something, Anna?"

Anna stood firm and said, "I surely hope so." She then explained her dilemma. Anna told her that she didn't think Mrs. Schultz believed her story about Clay Mitchell, and that she was truly sorry for being late to class. She hoped she wouldn't receive a demerit. She waited until Mrs. Heinrich made a call to Mrs. Schultz's classroom to verify what she'd been told. Anna was almost sure that more wrath was going to be heaped on her.

But to her surprise, Mrs. Heinrich appeared to be understanding, and even forced a little smile at Anna.

"Anna, your story appears to be true, so I'm going to excuse you <u>this</u> time, but you must not let this happen again. Understood? I will also speak to Clay Mitchell and make sure he does not do this again, to <u>any</u> student."

Anna heaved a big sigh of relief and was about to thank Mrs. Heinrich, when the woman spoke again.

"You Jewish children must show some respect, and take responsibility for your actions."

Anna felt rage boiling inside her again. She was too angry to even cry. What in hell was wrong with these people? She wanted to go out into the courtyard of the school and scream, <u>Dammit, I'm not Jewish</u>! But she knew it wouldn't make any difference. She spun on her heels, without thanking Mrs. Heinrich, and left the office. She was trying to justify the provocation of that last statement, but she couldn't, any more than she could understand Mrs. Schultz's hateful reference to <u>you people</u>.

Anna was so thoroughly disgusted. She didn't know which was worse: the constant verbal abuse by her teachers, and remarks from students like, "You don't belong here," at least three to four times a week, or of her ethnic heritage. Or, going to her lockers in the main lobby and P.E. and finding big, ugly, painted Swastikas on the locker doors. Painted under the Swastikas were the words, "Leave, Jew." She realized that these students were getting giddy, passing out this kind of persecution, and that it would continue as long as she was in that school. She wondered what kind of parents permitted this form of abusive behavior. Her father would kill her if he ever found her doing anything like that. The locker doors were always cleaned after school, only to have the Swastikas reappear a day or two later.

The worst part was, to whom could she go? Whom could she tell to make it stop? She had no one. Not the teachers or anyone in Administration, and she couldn't go to the Principal. That meant going through channels, and she knew she'd never get to see him. She thought of telling her parents, but was afraid to at this time. After all, she'd only been in school for two weeks. So, she decided to <u>never be alone</u>. Not in P.E. class, and not in the cafeteria, and certainly not in the halls of the school. She would always be part of a group, going to class, etc. Though she succeeded in keeping herself <u>safe</u>, there were some students who didn't want her around them.

On Wednesday of the second week, she and four other freshman students were blindfolded and forced to swallow de-shelled garden snails attached to a string. This was really a horrible thing, and it was incomprehensible to Anna that the school allowed this.

The freshmen were told the snails were raw oysters and wouldn't hurt them. Once they swallowed, the string was then pulled back and out through their mouths, whereupon they immediately vomited in front of God and everyone. Then, the incredibly cruel Upper Classmen told the freshmen what they really swallowed. To the delight and laughter of all those around them, the freshmen vomited again.

Her freshman year had begun horribly. She was constantly scared, suspicious of everyone, distrustful of other students, and looked like someone dressed from a charitable grab-bag. When she dropped a few hints about her circumstances to distant friends, no one believed her. She knew she'd have the same response from her parents. Her father would not even comprehend such a thing. He was so strict that he would certainly believe that Anna had somehow instigated this whole scenario. Why? Because, to her knowledge, this sort of thing never remotely happened to either her father or mother at any time. That was the scariest part of all--she couldn't go to anyone.

CHAPTER FIVE

During the course of her stay at that high school, many things wounded Anna, both mentally and physically. She hated her Physical Education class. Again, she had a female German teacher named Miss Herman. This teacher looked like she had walked right out of a U.S. Marine poster. She had so many muscles on her body she resembled an over-sized body builder. Anna thought her to be the least feminine individual she had ever seen. She also had a loud, rasping voice like a Marine drill instructor, and was always yelling at everyone about something. Anna instantly had the feeling Miss Herman hated her on sight.

One day, during a field hockey game, Anna got hit by a hockey puck right in the front of her mouth.

It cut both her upper and lower lips, and knocked out one of her permanent front teeth. Did the game stop? Of course not. The girl who hit the puck was not even playing in the game. She had aimed the puck she was using straight at Anna, who was about eight feet away. Anna knew that <u>this</u> time, the act was very deliberate. She was so frightened, she screamed that she wanted to call her father to come and get her. Anna had blood all over her. Her mouth was swimming in it, and her P.E. clothes were all blood-spattered. Even the hockey puck had her blood all over it.

Miss Herman pulled Anna to the side of the field, looked at her open bloody mouth and said, "Don't worry, dentists do wonderful things these days. I don't think your lips need any stitches. Go wash out your mouth and come back to the game."

The idea of going home at that time was totally out of the question. Anna knew that if this had happened to any of the other girls, she would have been dismissed immediately. Not only that, nothing was said to the girl that had hit the puck at Anna. The psychological effect that this had on Anna was terrible. How could she be <u>so</u> hated, when the majority of the school's students didn't even know her? This was happening because they thought that she was Jewish? How frightening! She couldn't leave until after the class was over. Her father immediately took her to their dentist, and she was fitted with a partially capped tooth that was temporary, until a permanent false tooth could be fitted into her mouth.

The only thing Anna enjoyed in P.E. was the twice-weekly one-hour hygiene class for "preparedness," as Miss Herman called it. The required medical books had pictures of the male and female human anatomy. These books informed the students about sex, and how babies were conceived and born-- among other things. The information was mostly about cleanliness, and how it was possible to not only get pregnant, but also get a venereal disease as well. Anna loved that class, and the books. She couldn't believe how misinformed she had been. She remembered how evasive her mother had been when her menstrual periods had begun at the age of eleven. Her mother had never forewarned her about this, and when it happened at a Saturday afternoon movie with friends, Anna was horrified. She thought she was bleeding to death. At home, her mother apologized, then explained that this happens to all girls and not to be frightened about it.

"But, don't let a boy kiss you," she said, "because now you could get pregnant."

Can you believe this? But at age eleven, poor little vulnerable and misinformed Anna <u>did</u> believe it. Her parents had never discussed sex, romance, or the equivalent, in her presence at any time. It just wasn't done--at least not in her family. So when she "fell in love" for the first time in the seventh grade, her parents did everything possible to keep them apart outside of school, and were positively delighted when he and his family moved out of state.

So now, no more hygiene class. Her father became livid when he saw the books Anna was reading and told Miss Herman that he believed she was "trying to encourage her female students to become promiscuous." Then, in front of everyone in the class, he shoved the books into Miss Herman's hands and told her that Anna would go to her study hall class instead of hygiene. He'd talked to the principal and it was already arranged.

It was the first time that Miss Herman's students saw her speechless. Her mouth hung open. She just glared at Anna's father, then turned her back on him. So now, to get even, she was going to take out her anger on Anna. She made Anna participate in P.E. classes every day, even though Anna had a written doctor's order that she not participate in sports for two weeks during her monthly menstrual cycle. The doctor wasn't sure what made Anna have such lengthly periods, but he did order NO SPORTS ACTIVITIES during this time.

Anna kept maintaining her silence about her continued harassment and discrimination at school. Twice, during class, she bled through her clothes and was again forced to call her father to come and get her from school. She was the only student in that P.E. class that had this kind of treatment from her teacher. Their doctors' requests were always honored.

Her father finally, partly in desperation, asked, "Do you want to see this doctor again?"

"No!" Anna practically screamed.

Miss Herman's reaction to all of this was pure belligerence. She continued to ignore Anna's doctor's written orders, and accused Anna of being a pansy, and stated that "Jewish people always have loads of excuses for everything."

During that first year, Anna wasn't allowed to play after-school sports, where the teams would board their high school bus and go to another out-of-town school. Even though her parents were strict about her activities, they permitted Anna to participate. She loved baseball so much, and was an excellent first-baseman.

But she was never allowed to go.

She tried to decide whether it was just pure hatred of her personally, or that maybe they were ashamed of having someone of her mistaken race with them. Like Cinderella, she was treated like a worthless individual and had to stay home. Unfortunately, Anna didn't have a fairy godmother to assist her with this problem.

The P.E. hour also had a dance class once a week, and the boys' gym were invited over to participate as dancing partners. They did the current dancing of that time: Jitterbug, Swing, Waltz, Foxtrot, and Square dancing. Anna was the best female dancer in the group, and was told so by all of her classmates. Even Miss Herman begrudgingly admitted so. A very nice boy, Paul Wilson, also a fabulous dancer, always asked to team with Anna as his partner. They danced so wonderfully together, and pretty much led the rest of the class. But when it came time at the end of the first semester to put on the Showtime for the teachers, students and parents, Anna was replaced as Paul's partner and not allowed to take part in the Showtime at all. Anna again wondered if it were her race, or Miss Herman getting even?

At any rate, she chose not to tell her parents of the event, because they would go and then ask her why she wasn't in the show. This time Anna was really heartbroken. She finally crumpled under the constant, horrible persecution that was always put upon her and cried her eyes out.

Then, to her great surprise, a few days later she found out that Paul wouldn't dance without her at the show, and that he had also been replaced. She was absolutely ecstatic. His wonderful support and thoughtfulness compensated for a lot of agony. Only God knew how enormously grateful she was that her freshman year would soon be over.

CHAPTER SIX

Through all of this oppressive time, Anna had so much trouble concentrating on her studies, she had come very close to failing her freshman year. She was failing math due to incomplete homework, she was failing English because she had not read nor submitted book reports on the five assigned books. She had to be tutored for math, and much to the anger of her teacher, she did make up her homework and passed the class with a 'C'. As for world history and Latin, she got "Cs" in those classes also. She loved world history, but couldn't give it the time that she wanted. Now, she was so fearful of failing English that she stiffened her scared little spine and took her chances with talking to her teacher, Mrs. Griffith.

Mrs. Griffith was tall and stately, with a gentle manner and lovely face. Her beautiful soft green eyes spoke volumes. She was Anna's only non-German teacher out of five classes.

Anna did her best to explain her situation to Mrs. Griffith, keeping the worst to herself, and apologized immensely for her negligent participation in class. She took a deep breath and asked Mrs. Griffith if she, Anna, could make up the five required book reports during the summer vacation so that she wouldn't fail English and flunk her freshman year. Anna was so afraid she would be refused. She didn't know what she would do if that happened. She just had not been able to handle all of that homework on those other heavy classes, and absorb all of the unwarranted persecution at the same time. It was getting hopelessly impossible, but she was still afraid to tell her parents of her predicament.

Mrs. Griffith was always aware that something was troubling Anna, and thought that Anna's problems might be related to family. She was totally wrong.

Feeling sorry for her, Mrs. Griffith agreed to the summer routine, but only after talking to Anna's parents first.

Mrs. Griffith was so kind and understanding when talking to Anna's mother and father, and told them that she knew Anna had appeared stressful and sometime sickly on many days in her class. She told them that she had been disappointed that Anna's work was not completed at year's end, and though the parents appeared stern and worried, they agreed to the summer arrangement. After all, what choice did they have? They certainly didn't want her to fail her freshman year. Her father kept looking over at Anna during the discussion, and made a mental note to speak to her about the neglect of her English studies.

After Mrs. Griffith left, he took Anna into his den and asked her to please sit down and tell him what had been going on. What had required summer make-up courses in one of her studies?

"Why couldn't you read and produce the book reports on time? And don't lie to me, Anna, I want the truth. I can't advise if I don't know the truth."

Anna didn't know where to begin, but she did know she couldn't possibly tell him the whole truth. At least, not yet. Her father's temper was something to be very cautious of, and she couldn't afford to tell him now, with the year almost over. She was truly between a rock and a hard spot. In a sense, she was proud of herself for sticking it out and managing to steel herself against the unwarranted intolerance shown her this past year on campus. She had decided that all of this cruel animosity would pass before her sophomore year began.

"Dad, you know that I don't come to you about my homework, so you have no way of knowing how much I have, or how hard it is. Just like math--I could hardly get through that class, and even had to be tutored to pass it. That's why Mrs. Griffith said that sometimes I looked stressed and sickly. I am, sometimes, from worry about it all. And freshman year has been no picnic! It was hard to get used to. I don't see any of my friends, and I'm lonesome for them. I promise that I'll try to do better." Anna sat back in her chair, hating herself for lying like that. She watched her father watch her, while he quietly smoked his cigarette. He was so old-fashioned, so there was a very good chance that if he had known about her terrible situation, he wouldn't believe it, and she would be blamed for not participating in her studies like she should have. Since her heritage was old and honorable, and, since he'd never experienced the persecution of "being Jewish", he would have a hard time understanding what she was going through.

"You're sure that's all there is to this?" he asked Anna.

"I swear, Dad, I'll pick up the slack and get good grades on those book reports. I promise!" God, she hated to continue lying like that, but felt if she could just get through her freshman year, everything would be okay. She'd gotten through that horrible week of Initiation, hadn't she? Heaven forbid, if she told him about being blindfolded and being forced to swallow garden snails, he would really have come apart. That was one of the worst things that she'd had to endure during initiation. Carrying all of those extra books was bad, but not as bad as eating snails!

Anna, forever grateful to Mrs. Griffith for her kindness and assistance, did make up all of her five book reports that summer, and received good grades for each one. She found that the reading and writing of the book reports weren't so bad. She loved to read, and it enabled her to finally relax and enjoy her three-month summer vacation. She was even able to manage a few days at the beach with her family, and even acquired a very nice tan.

CHAPTER SEVEN

Then, the dreaded beginning of her sophomore year at the same high school was upon her. She still hadn't told her parents of her daily stress and abuses during the previous year, and all of the hateful things that she had been subjected to. She was hoping that all of that was in the past. She definitely knew, that as an upper classman herself, she would be so helpful to any freshman who needed her. She couldn't imagine treating anyone as she had been treated, regardless of their race. She promised herself that if she was present at any of these abusive occurrences, that she would do her best to stop it.

Now, she was just praying that everyone on campus was used to seeing her and having her around, and that her teachers would be kinder in her sophomore year.

Well, her prayers went unanswered.

She had different teachers, but that didn't matter. She also had different courses. She was finally taking the business courses that she so badly wanted. And another BIG surprise: She finally realized, after a whole miserable year, that there were only Caucasian and Hispanic students on campus at this school, which she thought of as being very unusual. She thought back to her freshman year and remembered she had never met or seen any other Middle Eastern students, nor any African-American or Asian students, which was very strange. But then, she had been so self-absorbed in her own daily problems, it had been easy to overlook. So, she entered her sophomore year, still being hated by the German teachers and many ignorant students.

Anna reflected on her freshman year. She had made a few nice friendships on campus, but nothing that would sustain her during her time at this school. Some of her classmates wanted to be friends with her, but were fearful of reprisals. It really was a terrible situation. She had survived so much: Initiation, and looking as ugly as Sin during that week, and putting up with more hateful prejudice and ignorance than could be imagined in a supposed civilized world. She remembered the Swastikas on her lockers, and on her book covers, which she changed almost daily with fresh grocery brown paper bags, that her parents never saw. Add to that, the pushing and shoving she endured for no particular reason, which caused skinned knees, hands and elbows. She never did know who was responsible. She endured verbal abuses by the teachers and the adults in the school whom she should have been able to go to when her heavy cross got too hard to carry. For the life of her, she couldn't understand why being Jewish was so terrible. God was a Jew, wasn't He? Yeah, well look what happened to Him!

She made up her mind that if more persecution followed her into her sophomore year, she would just do her best to ignore it. She remembered saying about a thousand times, "I'm not Jewish, I'm Egyptian," to no avail. Thank God that first year was past, and hopefully, never to be repeated.

Nice try, Anna, but NO SUCH LUCK! The outrageous and ridiculous jeering of "Hey, Jew, you here again?" followed her right into her sophomore year, along with the same Swastikas back on her locker doors. Anna kept telling herself that she could handle it.

CHAPTER EIGHT

At the end of the first month of school, a talent show was organized by the upper classmen, and all those who had any talent in playing a musical instrument, dancing, singing, reading poetry, etc., were invited to participate. Anna's very best friend in the whole world, Susie Powell, approached Anna and wanted the two of them to sing in the show. Susie and Anna had been like sisters since <u>before</u> first grade, and had participated in many musical shows including grade school, church, and some womens' clubs. Their best and most chosen performance was singing a duet of "Sentimental Journey". Anna would sing soprano, and Susie, alto. Susie had already asked a female upper classman to accompany them on the piano, and was so excited about this.

Susie was everything that Anna wasn't: curly blond hair; beautiful big blue eyes; an extrovert in every sense of the word. Even though she was about fifteen pounds overweight, on her it looked good.

The problem was, Anna had not told Susie of her dreadful experiences on campus the previous year, and she wasn't planning on doing so now. She tried to argue with Susie, saying, "They weren't good enough for this show," and, "The students would laugh at them," and finally telling her that she, Anna, was too shy to sing in front of so many people. She tried everything she could think of to dissuade Susie, but nothing worked.

Susie listened to all of Anna's tirade. Very quietly she said, "Don't be such a chicken, and quit trying to tell me that we're not good enough. That makes me mad, and you know better. You also know that we can do this very well, as always. So stop your complaining and shape up. We'll go see our accompanist tomorrow, and set up practice dates."

Anna tried to tell herself that their accomplished duet would be joyfully accepted as usual. Then, on the day of the show, she realized she'd made a horrible mistake.

The audience consisted of approximately eight-hundred persons: students, teachers, and administrative employees. The duet, "Sentimental Journey", was sung beautifully, and when finished, the auditorium was still as death. Then finally, a few handclaps from teachers, and possibly some freshmen students, but that was all. Then a tomato came flying onto the stage and hit the side of the piano. Someone in the audience yelled, "You're dirtying the stage, Jew. Get off!"

Susie was dumbstruck. She couldn't comprehend what was happening. She didn't even acknowledge the audience. She just ran off the stage, hysterically sobbing.

Anna followed her backstage and tried to calm her down, but was at a loss herself. She and Susie had sung their song beautifully, and she hated having her wonderful friend exposed to the nasty verbal and abusive treatment that she'd been experiencing the past year and beginning of <u>this</u> year.

Susie finally calmed down a little and asked, "What is this <u>Jew </u>crap? Did you mistakenly tell anyone in school you were Jewish?"

Anna sat on the floor backstage, and put her head in her hands. "Of course not. My large Egyptian nose and my different appearance is being mistaken for Jewish! I've said a thousand times, all last year, 'I'm not Jewish, I'm Egyptian and Catholic'. But do you think they believe me? Even my teachers are unbelieving. Look at me. I don't look like anyone else on campus. I'm different, so I'm scum. That's what Jews are supposed to be, I guess. These people are crazy! I don't know what to do, and I don't have anyone here at school that I can go to for help. Did you see any teacher try to find out who threw that tomato at us?"

Susie looked down at Anna with stern but loving eyes. "That's crap!" she said. Susie loved that word. "There's got to be someone you can go to. Have you told your parents about this?"

Anna looked forlorn. "No, I haven't, I can't yet. I'm afraid. I don't think that Dad will understand. I've only told three people in P.E. class, because they've seen what's going on. Even they don't completely grasp this terrible situation I'm going through. They're sympathetic, probably because they're not German. But they can't help in any way! As far as Dad is concerned, he's liable to think that I'm doing this for attention since he and Mom have never experienced anything like this--at least not to my knowledge." Anna did feel much better now that she had confided her troubles to her best friend, but felt so bad that this horrid abuse had affected Susie.

Anna looked up at her. "I'm so sorry, Suz. This is why I was trying to back out of the show. I was afraid something would happen. And it did! I should have told you. Please forgive me for putting you through this."

Susie pulled Anna to her feet. "Don't be ridiculous, and don't apologize for something you have absolutely no control over. There's just no accounting for stupidity. All I can say is, these people are really sick and ignorant! Screw 'em. Let's go get a malt!"

CHAPTER NINE

Anna tried to maintain her courage and ignore what was repeating itself, but found herself afraid all over again. This time, it was impossible to condone the abuses put upon her. When she had food thrown at her between classes, she decided enough was enough.

After four more sophomore months of pure anguish, she got extremely ill. She couldn't keep her food down and was losing a lot of weight. She finally gave up the daily chore of pretense. The anxiety and depression of her ordeals finally overwhelmed her, and affected her health, her studies, her relationships with friends, and her family. Anna knew she would never understand what she was being subjected to, and why. She just knew that something in our society was horribly wrong, and wondered if it would ever be fixed. She was finally forced to tell her parents of her terrible continued abuses by teachers and students, beginning with Freshman Initiation. She feared telling her parents, but had no choice. They also had an inkling that something was very wrong, and were worried that Anna was very sick. But why?

Anna had so hoped that the discrimination against her would subside in her sophomore year. She told her parents that her miserable situation forced her to read and acknowledge books and articles relating to Germany, Adolph Hitler's horrific reign, World War II, and the attempts and successes of Jewish annihilation during the Holocaust. Reading about the horror that had befallen the Jews during that time made her ill, especially when reading about the death camps that mutilated and gassed people--even babies. It was very difficult to imagine that kind of hate.

Then, when remembering all of the unwarranted, unconscionable things that had happened to her in the past one and a half years, she wondered what kind of parents these miserable kids had. How much did these parents influence their teenagers to believe and support the atrocities that she'd read about? And how about her bigoted teachers? Did any one of them know or care about Anna and the fact she was non-Jewish? That fact was totally ignored.

After literally spewing out all of the hurt from her mind and heart, she finally asked her parents about <u>her</u> thoughts regarding these students and their parents. They couldn't answer her, but they did believe everything that she'd told them, through her tears of anguish.

CHAPTER TEN

Listening to Anna, her parents were absolutely stunned by what she had been forced to submit to. They could hardly believe she had kept all of this a secret for so long, and that it nearly destroyed her health. Her father was furious, and though he thought some of the things Anna said were possibly <u>questionable</u>, immediately took charge of the situation.

"For God's sake, Anna, what made you not only put up with this pathetic garbage, but keep it to yourself and not tell us? We should have known about this from the very beginning. And believe me, none of it would have happened. Of that you can be sure!"

"My hero," Anna thought, but didn't say it. Instead, she said, "I'm a grown girl, and tried not to be a baby about this and handle it myself. I just didn't realize how bad it could get. Besides, I really didn't think you'd believe me. But consider this: who could possibly make all of this stuff up?"

"You are not an adult, Anna, and even an adult would have trouble acknowledging this type of persecution. This situation has to be corrected. God only knows how many others have suffered through this, and how many are going to follow. The war is over, and no one wants the beginnings of a Holocaust here!"

The very next day, Anna's father went to the high school and confronted the principal of all that he'd learned, regarding the previous horrendous events directed at his daughter during her freshman year--and the first semester of her sophomore year. He had to explain that he was just now informed of this by his daughter, who had mistakenly thought she could handle all of this persecution alone. He had a difficult time talking about and dealing with the fact that the school permitted <u>any</u> of its upper classmen to force his daughter to eat garden snails; to be pushed downstairs; to ruin her back carrying ten books at a time; to serve others; to have Swastikas painted on her lockers constantly, and finally, to put up with continued verbal abuses by her teachers.

Anna had been pulled from her P.E. class to go to the principal's office. When she opened the front doors of the administration building, she heard her father in the principal's office. He was yelling, "Who the hell do you think you are?" She decided to stay just outside the door until she was called in. She heard her father threaten the school with newspaper coverage and a lawsuit. He was furious that his daughter's medical requests had been ignored by the P.E. teacher, and that this same teacher permitted Anna to lose a permanent front tooth due to racial dislike by other students. He ended his forceful tirade by calling Anna into the principal's office and telling her to acknowledge to the principal everything he'd said to be true. He then demanded the school to "Immediately release Anna from their so-called <u>Educational Facility</u>."

The principal appeared shocked by all of this news, and didn't even try to explain that he knew nothing about any of this--probably because he wasn't German. Nor did he attempt to apologize for this unholy situation.

Anna was released immediately and emptied her lockers, packed up her gym clothing, and left with her father. She later learned that she had a whole three-week reprieve from school because she was so far ahead in her studies. She was really elated with this news. So, after that refreshing time at home, relaxing and rejuvenating her spirits, her father placed her into a different high school, in a different town just fifteen miles from the original high school. There, one could actually SEE every other race of our society on that campus, and everyone getting along beautifully. It was so wonderfully NORMAL.

CHAPTER ELEVEN

After one and a half miserable, misunderstood years, Anna was welcomed as part of this fantastic Student Body. She received enormous support from her counselors and teachers, and finally felt the freedom she had so yearned for, but not without sadly fearing for other Jewish or Middle Eastern students at that time, at that place.

The difference of the two high schools couldn't even be explained. It seemed almost impossible that they were only fifteen miles apart, but yet so unbelievably different. Almost as if they were on different planets. If there were any Jewish students on THIS campus, and Anna was sure there were, no one knew who they were. Or cared. Their race and religion weren't important to anyone.

The current high school made it possible for Anna to choose and belong to the academic class clubs that she chose, and even belong to and sing in the fabulous school choir, which she loved. She excelled in after-school sports, and even won some awards during her Girls Athletic Association years.

Anna graduated from this wonderful high school in 1949, with cheering from classmates, friends and family. She knew that she'd accomplished a great deal in the last two and a half years in this school. But more importantly, she'd endured a phase of her life that was cruel, demeaning, and sometimes violent. She prayed that, with God's help, it would never happen again, to any student in the United States.

EPILOGUE

Later in my life, 1982, my husband and I moved to northern Idaho, totally unaware of the current status of the Aryan Nation.

One day, on a warm summer afternoon, I was at a filling station putting gasoline into our car. Out of nowhere, two young blond men, each about eighteen or nineteen, came up and stood beside me. Both men were holding Zippo lighters. When I turned to them, they clicked the lighters; flames shot several inches high and they stuck them in my face. I jumped back and screamed. The boys rushed to their car and took off, tires screeching as they sped out of the driveway. The owner of the station ran out to me.

"Damned bunch of punks!" he said, staring after them.

That kind of intimidation on one who is totally unsuspecting is very frightening. I later learned the Aryan Nation's philosophy is, "Dark hair, dark eyes, and a toned complexion have no place in America. America belongs to WHITE POWER!" Unfortunately, these people have taken over a good portion of Idaho as well as other states, and they are absolute cowards. To quote a very prominent civil rights lawyer, Morris Dees, "They are cesspool vigilantes!"

FOREWORD

POPULAR ANTI-SEMITISM:

During the 19th Century, anti-Jewish sentiments and stereotypes underwent changes. Rejection and discrimination of Jews was no longer based on religious differences alone. By the time the term <u>anti-Semitism</u> was first used in the late 1870s, Jews in Western Europe, although citizens with equal rights, were seen by may as alien to the nation or the people.

Since the beginning of the century, the notion has become popular that a people or nation is not a collection of individuals, but a unique organism created by climate, landscape and traditions. Those ideas, influenced mainly by the German Romantic Movement, repudiate the basic tenets of the enlightenment of common humanity and equality. In this view, Jews appear as alien intruders who need to be removed from the body of the nation.

The distinction between 'the people' or 'the nation' and those who are felt not to belong to it, is used more generally to stigmatize everything as 'Jewish' that is seen as negative or undesirable. For many, a 'Jew' becomes the epitome of weakness, bad character and ugly appearance--the negative mirror image of all the positive characteristics embodied in the people or nation.

Many of the new stereotypes develop on the background of industrialization and urbanization. These rapid social and economic changes are the source of great friction and conflict in society and come to be experienced by many as destructive and unnatural. As Jews emerge from their restricted positions and take up new opportunities, they are often identified as the force behind these developments. Thus, the stereotype of the Jew as the exploiter and usurer who profits from the loss of others is brought into the modern world, as is the myth of the all-powerful 'Jewish Conspiracy' capable of bending the course of the world to its own will and profit.

THE BIG 'SIX'. ARE THEY CAUSES OR EXCUSES? HOW CAN WE TELL THE DIFFERENCE?

1. Economic:

    We hate Jews because they possess too much wealth and power.

2. Chosen People:

    We hate Jews because they arrogantly claim they are the chosen people.

3. Scapegoat:

Jews are a convenient group to single out and blame for our troubles.

4. Deicide:

We hate Jews because they killed Jesus.

5. Outsiders:

We hate Jews because they are different than us.

6. Racial Theory:

We hate Jews because they are an inferior race.

Many people have claimed that Jews as a group possess far too much wealth and power. We call this the Economic Theory of anti-Semitism. It postulates that Jewish wealth and power arouses the envy of other groups, and this in turn leads to anti-Semitism. This theory has surfaced in different guises throughout history. One of the ways it became popularized was through 'The Protocols of the Elders of Zion.'

This is a vicious anti-Semitic book. It is the second most widely published book in history. The book is a complete fabrication, created by the Russian secret police. It is an alleged record of the minutes of a secret meeting held by Jewish leaders. These influential Jews, said the book, were plotting to take over the entire world. This fictional account provided an excellent excuse for the Russians to intensify their campaign of oppression against the Jews. It also strongly influenced the masses and bolstered the credibility of the myth that Jews control governments. Do people today still believe that Jews have some mysterious financial and organizational advantage over the rest of humanity? Read 'The Protocols' and decide for yourself.

WHY PEOPLE SHOULD STUDY AND REMEMBER THE HOLOCAUST:

The Holocaust is not just a word used to describe something anymore. It is spelled with a capital 'H' and is known to everyone as Tragedy.

We should study the Holocaust because it teaches us about prejudice.

We should learn about the Holocaust because we want to, not because we have to.

We should study the Holocaust to learn how cruelly the Jews were treated for just being human.

We should study the Holocaust because there is no doubt it could start again.

We should study the Holocaust to prevent future ones.

We should study the Holocaust to be grateful for the things we have.

We owe it to the innocent people who died, for the people tortured in concentration camps, and also for the people who escaped and saw their loved ones dying at their feet.

We should study the Holocaust so that people at a young age can learn and not repeat the mistakes of the past when they grow up. The gas chambers, concentration camps and forced labor are all things one should know about.

Many people probably said to themselves, "They aren't coming for me. Why should I care?" Well, I can answer that with another question: "What if they came for you? Who will be around to help then?"

I really think our country should have helped more, but we didn't. We could have saved many lives.

Finally: We should study the Holocaust so that our outer self does not blind us!

<u>LAST BY NOT LEAST</u>:

Find a computer and <u>SEARCH</u> for "Holocaust Resources.com"

Re: Teaching Holocaust Studies with the Internet

Women and the Holocaust WebQuest

Holocaust WebQuest

About the Holocaust

Anti-Semitism

The United States Holocaust Museum

And there are so many more. It is my hope that these resources help in the study of humanity and inhumanity, with the goal of adding to your understanding of human behavior and making you more sensitive human being.

Attorney Morris Dees, is a pioneer in using 'damage litigation' to fight hate groups.

Dee, co-founder of the Southern Poverty Law Center in Montgomery, Alabama, seeks to destroy hate by bankrupting them through civil lawsuits.

Speaking after an Idaho jury awarded punitive and compensatory damages to a woman and her son who were attacked by Aryan Nation guards, he said he seeks to own the copyright to the Aryan Nation's name and retire it, after winning a $6.3 million judgment against the Aryan Nation in September, 2000.

He is not unique in using the 'damage litigation' strategy to fight crime, but he is easily the best known. Under the strategy, Dees does not go after the individual perpetrators of hate crimes. Instead, he goes after the groups they belong to, in a bid to ruin them financially.

The lawsuit Dees argued successfully against the Aryan Nations is a case in point. The jury found that Aryan Nation's leader, Pastor Richard Butler, the group and its corporate entity, Saphire Inc., were negligent in overseeing the security guards who assaulted Victoria and Jason Keenan in 1998. The Keenans were chased, shot at and attacked after they stopped to search for a lost wallet outside the Aryan Nation's headquarters north of Coeur D'Alene, Idaho. The jurors deliberated about 10 hours over two days before setting $6 million as a 'punitive damage award' with $330,000.00 in 'compensatory damages; to the Keenans.

If the defendants cannot afford to pay the amount awarded against them, Dees seeks to force them to liquidate their assets. That way, experts say, Dees makes sure the victims are compensated, hate groups are put out of business, and he and the SPLC get paid.

Quoting Mr. Dees: "America is great because of its diversity--not in spite of it!"

ABOUT THE AUTHOR

The author is a 72-year-old Senior Citizen who lives and plays in Southern California. She loves Life, and prays to experience "so much more of it" before her time on Earth is ended.

She loves to read, write; and "shopping" is her favorite pasttime. She is very devoted to her loving husband, wonderful family -- and adores her three grandchildren.

In 1993, she studied for 2 years with the Childrens Institute of Literature, which was a very satisfying experience, and brought about the publication of "Impossible to Forget". She has also been published many times for her Poetry, which are included in various Anthologies.